T0083830

COUNTER-WAVE

COUNTER-WAVE

POETRY OF RESCUE IN
THE FIRST WORLD WAR

EDITED BY PAUL O'PREY

First published in Great Britain in 2018 by Dare-Gale Press
32 Loman Street,
London SE1 0EH

www.daregale.com

Information on the Copyright held by rights holders for individual
poems is listed in the Acknowledgements section on pages 142-143.
Introduction and this selection © Paul O'Prey 2018.
Front cover: 'Poilu and Tommy' painted by William Orpen in 1917,
© Imperial War Museums (Art.IWM ART 2959).

ISBN   9780993331138

Printed and bound in Great Britain by TJ International Ltd, Padstow

I see it all through a mist. It is misty but eternal. It is a scene in eternity, in some strange dream-hell where I am glad to be employed, where I belong, where I am happy. How crowded together we are here. How close we are in this nightmare. The wounded are packed into this place like sardines and we are so close to them... I've never been so close to human beings. We are locked together, the old ones and I, and the wounded men; we are bound together. We all feel it. We all know it. The same thing is throbbing in us, the single thing, the one life. We are one body, suffering and bleeding. It is a kind of bliss to me to feel this. I am a little delirious, but my head is cool enough, it seems to me.

Mary Borden
The Forbidden Zone

CONTENTS

Introduction

This collection brings together for the first time ten very different poets with the same remarkable story to tell, each in their own individual voice and from their own unique perspective.

When we talk of 'war poetry' we usually have in mind that extraordinary body of work by (mainly British) young male soldier-poets such as Wilfred Owen, Siegfried Sassoon, Robert Graves, and Isaac Rosenberg. The male and female poets in this collection also served at the Front, but not with a gun in their hand. The role they took upon themselves was to save life, not to take it. They were not engaged in the fighting, but had the terrible job of cleaning up after it. Like the soldier-poets, these volunteer aid workers wrote remarkable poems about what they saw and did. Their poems grapple with the same complex and disturbing emotions and they bear witness to the same ferocious brutality and suffering of war. But they also do something else.

It is perhaps best summed up by Mary Borden, the American nurse who wrote some of the most striking and extraordinary poems of the war. In one of her vivid prose 'sketches' written while she served at a field hospital on the Somme, she tells how she made it her business to create 'a counter-wave of life' against the overwhelming flood of suffering and death around her. She ran a field hospital of makeshift huts and tents close to the front line, in which she and her team (she founded the hospital at her own expense and ran it personally) treated 25,000 men in the first six weeks:

It was my business to sort out the wounded as they were brought in from the ambulances and to keep them from dying before they got to the operating rooms: it was my business to sort out the nearly dying from the dying. I was there to sort them out and tell how fast life was ebbing in them. Life was leaking away from all of them; but with some there was no hurry, with others it was a case of minutes. It was my business to create a counter-wave of life, to create the flow against the ebb. It was like a tug of war with the tide. The ebb of life was cold. When life was ebbing the man was cold; when it began to flow back, he grew warm.

Borden, a rich young woman in her twenties and the mother of three small children, put herself into situations of great hardship and danger, driven by a mission to help save as many lives as she could amidst the carnage of the Somme. Catching moments between the busy shifts that sometimes lasted twenty-four hours, she wrote poems and stories with a candor and passion that is reminiscent of Walt Whitman, who also tended the wounded on the battlefield, in his case during the American Civil War. In 'Unidentified', her most politically charged poem, she challenges the world's thinkers and moralisers to watch with her as a soldier dies in her care. She accuses them of betraying this 'ordinary man' who in life they would have looked down upon:

Look at him now. Look well, look long.

Your hungry brute, your ordinary man;

Your fornicator, drunkard, anarchist;

Your ruthless rough seed-sowing male;

Your angry greedy egotist;

Her lengthy description of the soldier as he dies is visceral and unflinching. Hers is the gaze of someone who saw too much but never looked away. Such a steady gaze into the face of violent death is famously found in Owen's harrowing account of recovering a soldier wounded in a gas attack, in his poem 'Dulce et Decorum Est'. In that poem Owen writes with the bold authority of a fellow soldier who has shared the wounded man's danger and experience. As a nurse, Borden has a different perspective to Owen, but she also claims the moment of a soldier's death, and her part in it, to write with an authority and directness that demands our attention, and that makes her one of the most compelling voices in the literature of war.

There are degrees of authority in writing about lived experience that depend on the poet's connection to or separation from a particular moment. In terms of war poetry, the soldier in the trench can say certain things that a civilian man or woman who only reads or hears about events second-hand might hesitate to express in a similar way. It was, for example, as a bystander that Laurence Binyon wrote what is perhaps the most famous war poem of all, composed after reading a newspaper article while on holiday at the very start of the war:

They shall grow not old, as we that are left grow old:
Age shall not weary them, nor the years condemn.
At the going down of the sun and in the morning
We will remember them.

These four lines created Binyon's reputation as the pre-eminent voice of a nation's collective grief, but they also typecast him as a certain sort of 'public' war poet which has diverted attention from his more personal and reflective work, particularly the poems written in the run up to and during the Second World War. 'For the Fallen' consciously reaches for the rhythms of the

King James Bible, the Book of Common Prayer and the plays of William Shakespeare, the most resonant of national texts to be drawn upon at a moment of great crisis. This is not to say that the poem does not express a deep or genuine emotion, and there is clearly a reason why these four lines are still read aloud at memorial services over one hundred years after they were written. But Binyon's tone changed after he experienced first-hand the realities of war, and after he came to realise the terrible extent of its inhumanity.

Binyon took time from his work as a curator at the British Museum to volunteer as a medical orderly at the 'English hospital' near Verdun, where John Masefield also worked for a time in the same role. It was a very physical job involving hard and dirty work, such as carrying the patients or incinerating amputated limbs after surgery. He became good friends with several of the French *poilus* ('tommies') and writes about them with tenderness and respect in poems of thoughtful reflection.

The arrangement of an anthology can often seem arbitrary, dependent perhaps on where an author happens to appear when sorted in terms of alphabetical order or date of birth. It seemed appropriate to me that the book should end with Laurence Binyon, as the oldest and perhaps most reflective of the ten poets brought together here. This then made it seem natural to start the collection with the brash youthfulness of Ernest Hemingway, who as an eighteen year-old was the youngest of these volunteer aid workers to go to the Front. His is the loud, rough new voice of a louder, rougher new century that Binyon struggled to adjust to. The collection therefore is arranged in order of the age at which a poet went to the war.

Like Hemingway, May Cannan and Carola Oman were also young when they went to France, both having only recently come of age. Cannan trained as a VAD (Voluntary Aid Detachment) nurse before the war but did not serve in that capacity at the Front. Instead she worked first in the famously busy 'Coffee Shop' canteen at the Rouen rail junction where soldiers were transferred by train to and from the front line, and then in Military Intelligence in Paris. The important morale role played by the Red Cross and other canteens in bringing comfort and support to soldiers is well documented by Laurence Binyon in *The Call and the Answer*, his prose account of a month-long journey along the Western Front in 1917, and Cannan's poem 'Rouen' brings vividly to life one such operation as she serves the men tea and sandwiches and watches them depart on the train, many of them never to return.

Carola Oman also trained as a VAD nurse at the start of the war, serving in England until she was old enough to be transferred abroad. Her carefully observed poems capture less well-documented moments, such as the British soldiers arriving in France who watch in silence as the leave ship passes them full of rowdy music and laughter, or the nurses who help to unload the ambulance train at midnight, or the atmosphere of resolute moral purpose in the Red Cross office.

There is a common assumption that war poetry at its best is always anti-war, though the reality is usually more complex and ambiguous than that. Even Owen and Sassoon, for all their hatred of the war, were highly competent and effective officers who won medals for their bravery in action. The writings of soldier poets reflect a wide range of views and attitudes to the war, and the same is true of the volunteer aid workers in this collection. Mary Borden, Vera Brittain, Laurence Binyon, Geoffrey Studdert Kennedy and John Masefield were all clearly driven by a deeply felt sense of duty to help as much as they could at a time of great humanitarian crisis. Ernest Hemingway and E.E. Cummings, both of whom volunteered as ambulance drivers, seem driven more by a sense of adventure.

Most of the poets seem to have supported the war at its outset, though several changed their views after experiencing the war first-hand. Geoffrey Studdert Kennedy, an army chaplain, was rather enthusiastic at the start of the conflict, but he later railed against the violence and inhumanity it unleashed and became critical of the political leadership that allowed it to happen. Writing in 1918 he denounced 'that power of sickly sentimentalism, that idiotic pomp and pageantry of militarism, which provide the glamour and romance for the mean and dirty shambles that are the battlefields of the world's great wars.' Vera Brittain, who was later to become a campaigner for pacifism, expresses the most bitter sense of betrayal at having sacrificed so much, in starkly unhappy poems such as 'The Lament of the Demobilised'.

May Cannan, on the other hand, warned about assuming that everyone shared the same journey from illusion to disillusion. In her memoir, *Grey Ghosts and Voices*, she wrote: 'A saying went round, "Went to the war with Rupert Brooke and came home with Siegfried Sassoon." I had much admired some of Sassoon's verse but I was not coming home with him.' She maintained belief in the cause for which she had volunteered, though it is true to say that she did not witness first-hand what

Binyon called 'the horrible slaughter' and 'the misery, the wasting and the maiming' of the trenches, which he came to know only too well.

Three of the ten poets in this collection are young American writers who have tended not to feature in standard anthologies of First World War poems. The work of Ernest Hemingway, E.E. Cummings and Mary Borden stands out for its energy, innovation and frankness compared to their British counterparts such as Masefield and Binyon, who went to France with well-established reputations and a way of writing that does not change.

Other older poets with an already established style include Geoffrey Studdert Kennedy and Robert Service, who both looked to Rudyard Kipling for a model of how to portray the common soldier with whom they felt a close bond. They were extremely popular writers whose dialect ballads ask us to heed the voice of the ordinary men they met at the Front and whose stories they wanted to tell. In several poems they write in the persona of an uneducated working-class soldier asked to risk everything but who stands to gain little in return. In their way these are very political poems and after the war Studdert Kennedy dedicated himself to supporting poor communities in Britain.

Hemingway can also seem to be adopting a persona and a voice that is not his own. His brusque, laconic poems read more like the bitter observations of a cynical, battle-hardened soldier, rather than the aid worker he actually was. Like Service, Hemingway was primarily a story-teller whose artistic impulse was to shape organic experience into more structured narratives, as he does in his novel about the war, *Farewell to Arms*. In his case the biographical context might suggest that there is also an element of personal myth-making in the poems.

Hemingway, Cummings and Borden were still developing their individual voices when they went to the Front. They were all profoundly affected by the war and their writing is being shaped by the world at the same time as they are discovering it. Cummings and Borden are both unrestrained in discarding poetic formalities and disrupting convention. This is not just about experimenting with form, but gives them a freedom to manoeuvre in managing extremely challenging subject matter. In the Preface to *The Forbidden Zone* (1929) Mary Borden pre-empts any complaint that readers might find her work confusing, saying that 'great confusion' was the very nature of the experiences she describes: 'Any attempt on my part to reduce them to order would require artifice on my part and would falsify them.' Borden had no wish to soften reality or impose artistic order and meaning onto an experience that by its nature had none.

These three American poets also address openly certain subjects that British poets may still have found taboo at the time, such as prostitution. In his later prose memoir *Goodbye To All That*, Robert Graves described the official organisation of red and blue-lamp brothels in a level of detail that his friend Sassoon thought distasteful, even in 1929. Graves did not, however, refer to such matters in the poetry he wrote at the time. Hemingway and Cummings had no such reticence, and Borden also touches on the subject of prostitution in the poem 'See how the withered leaves', in which women of the town find themselves driven to stand along the road 'where pleasure rides'.

While she was at the Somme Borden had an adulterous affair with Captain (later General) Louis Spears and the love poems she wrote to him are both passionate and intimate. In these poems, which were not published during her lifetime, she adopts a more traditional sonnet structure compared to her poems about the war. 'What more can the desolate murmuring sea' led to the ending of her marriage when discovered by her husband, who presumably took exception to its witty play on the famous Shakespearean *double-entendre* in which to die also means to orgasm. That she wrote it with death all around her, and with the prospect of the lovers' own violent death a daily possibility, gives this particular play on words an unsettling dimension.

Despite their differences of attitude and style, the ten poets in this collection are united by a sense of compassion and shared moral purpose. Their commitment to truthful witness, and their efforts to make sense of it all and seek hope in the face of despair, gives their poetry an authenticity that still resonates one hundred years after it was written. Together they form an important but still relatively untold part of the story of the First World War and its poetry.

Paul O'Prey

Ernest Hemingway

Ernest Hemingway was born in Oak Park, Illinois in 1899. He trained as a journalist on the *Kansas City Star* before volunteering as a driver with the American Red Cross ambulance service. He was sent to the Italian Front aged eighteen. His first job was to recover dead civilians from an exploded munitions factory. He also volunteered with a rolling (mobile) canteen, delivering cigarettes, chocolate and magazines to soldiers in the trenches by bicycle. While doing this at Fossalta di Piave in July 1918 he was badly wounded with multiple shrapnel and bullet wounds to both legs. He was awarded the Silver Medal of Military Valor for his 'admirable spirit of brotherhood' and for helping wounded Italian soldiers around him despite his own serious condition. Reports that he carried an Italian solder to safety on his back despite his own wounds were later contested.

Hemingway wrote a series of poems about the war, encouraged by Ezra Pound. It was as a novelist, however, that he was to make his name. *The Sun Also Rises* and *Farewell to Arms* draw on his experiences in the war and after. His later works include *For Whom the Bell Tolls* and *The Old Man and the Sea*. He was awarded the Pullitzer Prize and the Nobel Prize for Literature.

Captives

Some came in chains
Unrepentant but tired.
Too tired but to stumble.
Thinking and hating were finished
Thinking and fighting were finished
Retreating and hoping were finished.
Cures thus a long campaign,
Making death easy.

Champs d'Honneur

Soldiers never do die well;
Crosses mark the places,
Wooden crosses where they fell;
Stuck above their faces.
Soldiers pitch and cough and twitch;
All the world roars red and black,
Soldiers smother in a ditch;
Choking through the whole attack.

Killed   Piave – July 8 – 1918

Desire and
All the sweet pulsing aches
And gentle hurtings
That were you,
Are gone into the sullen dark.
Now in the night you come unsmiling
To lie with me
A dull, cold, rigid bayonet
On my hot-swollen, throbbing soul.

All armies are the same

All armies are the same
Publicity is fame
Artillery makes the same old noise
Valor is an attribute of boys
Old soldiers all have tired eyes
All soldiers hear the same old lies
Dead bodies always have drawn flies

Riparto d'Assalto

Drummed their boots on the camion floor,
Hob-nailed boots on the camion floor.
Sergeants stiff,
Corporals sore.
Lieutenants thought of a Mestre whore —
Warm and soft and sleepy whore,
Cozy, warm and lovely whore:
Damned cold, bitter, rotten ride,
Winding road up the Grappa side.
Arditi on benches stiff and cold,
Pride of their country stiff and cold,
Bristly faces, dirty hides —
Infantry marches, Arditi rides.
Grey, cold, bitter, sullen ride —
To splintered pines on the Grappa side
At Asalone, where the truck-load died.

To Good Guys Dead

They sucked us in;
King and country,
Christ Almighty
And the rest.
Patriotism,
Democracy,
Honor –
Words and phrases,
They either bitched or killed us.

The Age Demanded

The age demanded that we sing
and cut away our tongue.

The age demanded that we flow
and hammered in the bung.

The age demanded that we dance
and jammed us into iron pants.

And in the end the age was handed
the sort of shit that it demanded.

Carola Oman

Carola Oman began training as a VAD nurse in 1914, at the age of seventeen. She served during the war in hospitals in Oxford, Dorset and London, before being posted to France in September 1918, where she was stationed in Boulogne, Wimereux, and Terlingham. Her poems about the war were published in 1919 as *The Menin Road and Other Poems*, which was dedicated to four fellow VAD nurses, including May Wedderburn Cannan.

After the war she wrote many successful historical novels and biographies. *Sir John Moore,* her book about the British Army General who died fighting in the wars against Napoleon, won the James Tait Black Memorial Prize in 1953. She is best known for an acclaimed biography of Nelson, published in 1946, and for her retelling of the Robin Hood stories for children.

Unloading Ambulance Train

Into the siding very wearily
She comes again:
Singing her endless song so drearily,
The midnight winds sink down to drift the rain.
So she comes home once more.

Is it an ancient chanty
Won from some classic shore?
The stretcher-bearers stand
Two on either hand.
They bend and lift and raise
Where the doors open wide
With yellow light ablaze.
Into the dark outside
Each stretcher passes. Here
(As if each on his bier
With sorrow they were bringing)
Is peace, and a low singing.

The ambulances load,
Move on and take the road.
Under the stars alone
Each stretcher passes out.
And the ambulances' moan
And the checker's distant shout
All round to the old sound
Of the lost chanty singing.
And the dark seamen swinging.
Far off some classic shore...
So she comes home once more.

Night Duty in the Station

I
Slowly out of the siding the troop train draws away,
Into the dark it passes, heavily straining.
Shattering on the points the engine stutters.
Fires burn in every truck. Rich shadows play
Over the vivid faces… bunched figures. Someone
        mutters
'Rainin' again… it's raining.'

Slammings – a few shouts – quicker
Each truck the same moves on.
Weary rain eddies after
Drifts where the deep fires flicker.
Into the dark with laughter
The last truck wags… it is gone.

II
Horns that sound in the night when very few are
        keeping
Unwilling vigil, and the moonlit air
Is chill, and everything around is sleeping –
Horns that call on a long low note – ah, where
Were you calling me last?
The ghastly huntsman hunts no more, they say
The Arcadian fields are drugged with blood and clay.
And is Romance not past?

III
The station in this watch seems full of ghosts.
Above revolves an opalescent lift
Of smoke and moonlight in the roof. And hosts

Of pallid refugees and children, shift
About the barriers in a ceaseless drift.

Forms sleeping crowd beneath the rifle-rack,
Upon the bookstall, in the carts. They seem
All to be grey and burdened. Blue and black,
Khaki and red, are blended, as a dream
Into eternal grey, and from the back
They stagger from this darkness into light
And move and shout
And sing a little, and move on and out
Unready, and again, into the night.

IV
The windows in the Post Office are lit with olive gold.
Across the bridge serene and old
White barges beyond count
Lie down the cold canal
Where the lost shadows fall;
And a transparent city shines upon a magic mount.

Now fired with turkis blue and green
Where the first sunshine plays
The dawn tiptoes between
Waiting her signal from the woodland ways…

The Lower Deck

Into the harbour now the boat was come.
They bawled for passports from the smoking-room.
Darkness upon the lower deck lay dumb
While a few elbowed through the crowded gloom.

The canvas flapped, and a blank face or two
Fathomed a laugh; till through the silence came
A thresh of waters; and thick blackness drew
Away… And a bright boat passed like a flame.

Rowdy music, song and shout,
'It's the leave-boat goin' out.
Passin' us they are.
Goin' 'ome.
Goin' 'ome.'…

The murmur drifted like a dream
Mouth to mouth – a sudden gleam –
Till the voices died afar,
Till the thresh of waters drowned
All sounds to a single Sound.

Boat passed boat. And then again
Came sudden vision, splendid pain.
These were my sons. Ah, who shall know
Into what night I watched them go,
How each blank face was dear to me,
How kindly fell the evening rain?
And I could see – and I could see.

Room 17, BRCS Headquarters

Yours the heroic clouds, the scar
Of sunset, the ingenuous mist
Of country hills above the town;
The quay; the eternal khaki twist
Between the leave-boat and the *Gare*
Across the bridge; the mid-day swell
Of market carts that rattle down
The cobbles from the citadel.

Void in the dark I found the room.
Through the pale windows gleamed the sky.
There was no light below, but lights
Irrelevant. The wind was high,
The harbour blank. In driven gloom
The long express moved slowly out.

The room that overlooks the quay,
The watcher of a thousand nights,
That sees the way each man shall take,
And the last port that he shall make,
Sees neither Death nor Comedy
But Purpose and defeated Doubt.

★British Red Cross Service

Ambulance Train 30

A.T. 30 lies in the siding.
Above her cold grey clouds lie, silver-long as she.
Like a great battleship that never saw defeat
She dreams: while the pale day dies down
Behind the harbour town,
Beautiful, complete
And unimpassioned as the long grey sea.

A.T. 30 lies in the siding.
Gone are her red crosses – the sick that were her own.
Like a great battleship that never saw defeat
She waits, while the pale day dies down
Behind the harbour town,
Beautiful, complete...
And the Occupying Army boards her for Cologne.

In the Ypres Sector

You have left beauty here in everything,
And it is we that are both deaf and blind.
By coarse grass mounds here the small crosses rise
Sunk sideways in the ditch, or low inclined
Over some little stream where waters sing
By shell holes blue with beauty from the skies.

Even the railways cutting has kind shade
And colour, where the rusty wire is laid
Round the soft tracks. Because you knew them thus
The dark mouthed dug-outs hold a light for us.
And here each name rings rich upon our ears
Which first we learnt with sorrow and with tears.

Lost Winds of Winter

Dim rivers twisting down the marshy green
Meadows, low-spreading heavy bare-branched trees
Hung with faint mists, and light skies above these
And drowsy rain clouds sinking dark between,
You only are the faithful, the enduring.
Let us return to you. The long alluring
Sunlight of Spring is here again. We come
On broken wings to you. Receive us home
Here in your quiet breast all hopes immuring.

Pipes on the Quai Chanzy, Boulogne

(The Pipes call home.)
'Here is no trouble, here no weary waking.
Over the swarthy crags the clouds rest low.
Between grey rocks the silent rivers go
Dark on their way – the way that ye are taking.

Here there is ultimate silence. Here exists
Nothing but rain and weeping. The ravine
Is dim all day, and wet the moss between
The river banks, and hung with mourning mists.'

(The Men of Glencoe ask –)
'What shall we say in the Valley of Weeping?
The Shepherds of Etive – the first to go forth –
Are slain. They are sleeping.
Their brothers turn north.
Their battles are over. They are cold as the snow.
And widowed the Sisters that wait in Glencoe.'

(The Pipes reply –)
'O Children of Weeping, turned homeward in sorrow
The Shepherds of Etive have watched you go forth.
They live, and their strength is the sun of tomorrow.
They shall speak in the winds that shall welcome you
        north.
They are watching their flocks that are whiter than
        snow
And they dream of the Sisters that wait in Glencoe…'

May Cannan

May Wedderburn Cannan was born in 1893. Before the war she trained as a VAD nurse and organised the creation of a temporary hospital in Oxford, which was taken over by the Army in 1914. In 1915 she spent four weeks volunteering at a large and busy canteen for soldiers passing through the railhead at Rouen. In 1918 she joined the Espionage Section of the British Mission in Paris as a secretary and took the telephone call that broke the news of the Armistice in November.

Her first volume of poetry, *In War Time,* was published in 1917, followed by *The Splendid Days* in 1919. She was much affected by the death of her fiancé Major Bevil Quiller-Couch, who survived some of the worst of the fighting only to die in the flu pandemic that swept through Europe at the end of the war.

After the war she worked as a secretary at King's College London, and as an assistant librarian at the Athenaeum Club. A manuscript autobiography was discovered after her death and published as *Grey Ghosts and Voices* in 1976.

Rouen

Early morning over Rouen, hopeful, high, courageous
      morning,
And the laughter of adventure and the steepness of the
      stair,
And the dawn across the river, and the wind across the
      bridges,
And the empty littered station and the tired people
      there.

Can you recall those mornings and the hurry of
      awakening,
And the long-forgotten wonder if we should miss the way,
And the unfamiliar faces, and the coming of provisions,
And the freshness and the glory of the labour of the day?

Hot noontide over Rouen, and the sun upon the city,
Sun and dust unceasing, and the glare of cloudless skies,
And the voices of the Indians and the endless stream of
      soldiers,
And the clicking of the tatties, and the buzzing of the
      flies.

Can you recall those noontides and the reek of steam
      and coffee,
Heavy-laden noontides with the evening's peace to win,
And the little piles of woodbines, and the sticky soda
      bottles,
And the crushes in the 'Parlour', and the letters coming in?

Quiet night-time over Rouen, and the station full of
      soldiers,

All the youth and pride of England from the ends of all
     the earth;
And the rifles piled together, and the creaking of the
     sword-belts,
And the faces bent above them, and the gay,
     heart-breaking mirth.

Can I forget the passage from the cool white-bedded
     Aid Post
Past the long sun-blistered coaches of the khaki Red
     Cross train
To the truck train full of wounded, and the weariness
     and laughter,
And 'Good-bye, and thank you, Sister', and the empty
     yards again?

Can you recall the parcels that we made them for the
     railroad,
Crammed and bulging parcels held together by their
     string,
And the voices of the sergeants who called the Drafts
     together,
And the agony and splendour when they stood to save
     the King?

Can you forget their passing, the cheering and the
     waving,
The little group of people at the doorway of the shed,
The sudden awful silence when the last train swung to
     darkness,
And the lonely desolation, and the mocking stars
     o'erhead?

Can you recall the midnights, and the footsteps of
     night watchers,
Men who came from darkness and went back to dark
     again,
And the shadows on the rail-lines and the
     all-inglorious labour,
And the promise of the daylight firing blue the
     window-pane ?

Can you recall the passing through the kitchen door to
     morning,
Morning very still and solemn breaking slowly on the
     town,
And the early coastways engines that had met the ships
     at daybreak,
And the Drafts just out from England, and the day shift
     coming down ?

Can you forget returning slowly, stumbling on the
     cobbles,
And the white-decked Red Cross barges dropping
     seawards for the tide,
And the search for English papers, and the blessed cool
     of water,
And the peace of half-closed shutters that shut out the
     world outside ?

Can I forget the evenings and the sunsets on the island,
And the tall black ships at anchor far below our balcony,
And the distant call of bugles, and the white wine in
     the glasses,
And the long line of the street lamps, stretching
     Eastwards to the sea?

...When the world slips slow to darkness, when the
      office fire burns lower,
My heart goes out to Rouen, Rouen all the world
      away;
When other men remember I remember our
      Adventure
And the trains that go from Rouen at the ending of
      the day.

Lamplight

We planned to shake the world together, you and I
Being young, and very wise;
Now in the light of the green shaded lamp
Almost I see your eyes
Light with the old gay laughter; you and I
Dreamed greatly of an Empire in those days,
Setting our feet upon laborious ways,
And all you asked of fame
Was crossed swords in the Army List,
My Dear, against your name.

We planned a great Empire together, you and I,
Bound only by the sea;
Now in the quiet of a chill Winter's night
Your voice comes hushed to me
Full of forgotten memories: you and I
Dreamed great dreams of our future in those days,
Setting our feet on undiscovered ways,
And all I asked of fame
A scarlet cross on my breast, my Dear,
For the swords by your name.

We shall never shake the world together, you and I,
For you gave your life away;
And I think my heart was broken by the war,
Since on a summer day
You took the road we never spoke of: you and I
Dreamed greatly of an Empire in those days;
You set your feet upon the Western ways
And have no need of fame –
There's a scarlet cross on my breast, my Dear,
And a torn cross with your name.

The Armistice

In an office in Paris
The news came through over the telephone:
All the terms had been signed: the War was won:
And all the fighting and the agony,
And all the labour of the years were done.
One girl clicked sudden at her typewriter
And whispered, 'Jerry's safe', and sat and stared:
One said, 'It's over, over, it's the end:
The War is over: ended': and a third,
'I can't remember life without the war'.
And one came in and said, 'Look here, they say
We can all go at five to celebrate,
As long as two stay on, just for today'.

It was quite quiet in the big empty room
Among the typewriters and little piles
Of index cards: one said, 'We'd better just
Finish the day's reports and do the files'.
And said, 'It's awf'lly like Recessional,
Now when the tumult has all died away'.
The other said, 'Thank God we saw it through;
I wonder what they'll do at home today'.

And said, 'You know it will be quiet tonight
Up at the Front: first time in all these years,
And no one will be killed there any more',
And stopped, to hide her tears.
She said, 'I've told you; he was killed in June'.
The other said, 'My dear, I know; I know…
It's over for me too… My man was killed,
Wounded… and died… at Ypres… three years ago…
And he's my Man, and I want him', she said,
And knew that peace could not give back her Dead.

Paris, November 11, 1918

Down on the boulevards the crowds went by,
The shouting and the singing died away,
And in the quiet we rose to drink the toasts,
Our hearts uplifted to the hour, the Day:
The King – the Army – Navy – the Allies –
England – and Victory. –
And then you turned to me and with low voice
(The tables were abuzz with revelry),
'I have a toast for you and me', you said,
And whispered 'Absent', and we drank
Our unforgotten Dead.
   But I saw Love go lonely down the years,
   And when I drank, the wine was salt with tears.

Paris Leave

Do you remember, in Paris, how we two dined
On your Leave's last night,
And the happy people around us who laughed and sang,
And the great blaze of light.

And the big bow-window over the boulevard
Where our table stood,
And the old French waitress who patted your shoulder and
Told us that love was good.

(We had lingered so long watching the crowds that moved
In the street below,
And saying the swift dear things of Lovers newly met,
That she had guessed us so.)

I remember her smile, and the ring of your spurs
On the polished stair;
And the touch of your hand, and the clear November night,
And the flags everywhere.

I remember the Concorde, and the fountains' splash,
The black captured guns;
And the grey-haired men with their wives who wept and kissed, and
The lovers of their sons.

And the French girls with their poilus who linked their hands

To dance round us two,
And sang '*Ne passeront pas*', till one broke loose and flung
Her arms wide and kissed you.

She was all France that night, and you brave Angleterre,
The unfailing friend;
And I cried, 'Vive la France', and we told each other
        again
The War was at an end.

It was so hard to believe it was really won,
And the waiting past;
That the years wherein we knew death were under our
        feet,
And our Love crowned at last...

I remember most now the faces of the girls,
And the still, clear stars.
We said we were glad later lovers would never know
The bitterness of wars.

The lamp of the courtyard gate was bright on the old
Ribbons on your breast;
And the songs and the voices died down the boulevards.
You said that Love was best.

France

You also know
The way the dawns came slow
Over the railway stations out in France;
And you have seen the Drafts entrain
By the blurred lanterns in the rain,
And wept the True Romance.

You've also gone,
Dead tired, stumbling on,
Over the pavé when the day was born;
And weary beyond sleep lain down
And heard the clocks strike in the town,
Most young, and most forlorn.

And you have met
On lone roads in the wet
Field Batteries trotting North, and stood aside
And sent your heart with them to fight,
And ridden with them through the night
Until the pale stars died.

And you know too
How a man whistles through
The dark a line of some forgotten song;

You've seen the Leave Boat in, and then
Gone back to jest with broken men
Who once were swift and strong.

You know how black
The night sea tides surged back

On dock stones where the stretcher bearers kneeled;
And how the fog greyed the men's lips
And the red crosses of the ships,
And how the searchlights wheeled.

You've woke to see
Death hurtle suddenly
On to the hut roofs when the Gothas came;
And watched a man by Love possessed
Fight through to morning, and go West
Whispering his Girl's name.

Wherefore I know
That you will serve also
The living Vision men call Memory,
And hold to the brave things we said,
And keep faith with the faithful Dead –
And speak of France with me.

Women Demobilized

July 1919
Now must we go again back to the world
Full of grey ghosts and voices of men dying,
And in the rain the sounding of Last Posts,
And Lovers' crying —
Back to the old, back to the empty world.

Now are put by the bugles and the drums,
And the worn spurs, and the great swords they carried,
Now are we made most lonely, proudly, theirs,
The men we married:
Under the dome the long roll of the drums.

Now are the Fallen happy and sleep sound,
Now, in the end, to us is come the paying,
These who return will find the love they spend,
But we are praying
Love of our Lovers fallen who sleep sound.

Now in our hearts abides always our war,
Time brings, to us, no day for our forgetting,
Never for us is folded War away,
Dawn or sun setting,
Now in our hearts abides always our war.

E.E. Cummings

E.E. Cummings was born in Cambridge Massachusetts in 1894. In 1917, just after graduating from Harvard, he volunteered as a driver with the Norton-Harjes Ambulance Corps in France. He struck a rapport with ordinary French soldiers but fell out with the authorities. After relations with his commanding officer deteriorated, he and a close friend, William Slater Brown, were at first demoted from driving the ambulances to washing them, and then arrested after their letters home gave grounds for an accusation of espionage and pacifism. Cummings was repeatedly asked if he hated Germans, to which he would only reply 'I love the French very much'. He spent four months in a French prison, an experience described vividly and with characteristic lightness and irony in *The Enormous Room* (1922). After his release he was repatriated to the USA where he was drafted into the army, although he did not return to front line service in Europe.

As both a poet and painter his experiments with form drew on Cubism and Surrealism. There is a serious playfulness to his writing in which linguistic innovation is more than just a stylistic rebellion against the 'authority' of grammar, syntax and conventional structure. His poems are designed to look curious on the page and combine acute observation with a freedom of spirit that made him one of the most popular American poets of the twentieth century.

the bigness of cannon
is skilful,

but i have seen
death's clever enormous voice
which hides in a fragility
of poppies....

i say that sometimes
on these long talkative animals
are laid fists of huger silence.

I have seen all the silence
filled with vivid noiseless boys

at Roupy
i have seen
between barrages,

the night utter ripe unspeaking girls.

O sweet spontaneous
earth how often have
the
doting

    fingers of
prurient philosophers pinched
and
poked

thee
,has the naughty thumb
of science prodded
thy

    beauty   .how
often have religions taken
thee upon their scraggy knees
squeezing and

buffeting thee that thou mightest conceive
gods
    (but
true

to the incomparable
couch of death thy
rhythmic
lover

    thou answerest

them only with

            spring)

"next to of course god america i
love you land of the pilgrims' and so forth oh
say can you see by the dawn's early my
country 'tis of centuries come and go
and are no more what of it we should worry
in every language even deafanddumb
thy sons acclaim your glorious name by gorry
by jingo by gee by gosh by gum
why talk of beauty what could be more beaut-
iful than these heroic happy dead
who rushed like lions to the roaring slaughter
they did not stop to think they died instead
then shall the voice of liberty be mute?"

He spoke.   And drank rapidly a glass of water

it's jolly
odd what pops into
your jolly tête when the
jolly shells begin dropping jolly fast you
hear the rrmp and
then nearerandnearerandNEARER
and before
you can

!

& we're

NOT
(oh–
–i say

that's jolly odd
old thing,jolly
odd,jolly
jolly odd isn't
it jolly odd.

first she like a piece of ill-oiled
machinery does a few naked tricks

next into unwhiteness,clumsily
lustful,plunges—covering the soiled
pillows with her violent hair
(eagerly then the huge greedily

Bed swallows easily our antics,
like smooth deep sweet ooze where
two guns lie,smile,grunting.)

"C'est la guerre"i probably suppose,
c'est la guerre busily hunting
for the valve which will stop this.
as i push aside roughly her nose

Hearing the large mouth mutter kiss pleece

look at this)
a 75 done
this nobody would
have believed
would they no
kidding this was my particular

pal
funny aint
it we was
buddies
i used to

know
him lift the
poor cuss
tenderly this side up handle

with care
fragile
and send him home

to his old mother in
a new nice pine box

(collect

lis
-ten

you know what i mean when
the first guy drops you know
everybody feels sick or
when they throw in a few gas
and the oh baby shrapnel
or my feet getting dim freezing or
up to your you know what in water or
with the bugs crawling right all up
all everywhere over you all me everyone
that's been there knows what
i mean a god damned lot of
people don't and never
never
will know,
they don't want

to
no

my sweet old etcetera
aunt lucy during the recent

war could and what
is more did tell you just
what everybody was fighting

for,
my sister

isabel created hundreds
(and
hundreds)of socks not to
mention shirts fleaproof earwarmers

etcetera wristers etcetera,my

mother hoped that

i would die etcetera
bravely of course my father used
to become hoarse talking about how it was
a privilege and if only he
could meanwhile my

self etcetera lay quietly
in the deep mud et

cetera
(dreaming,
et
    cetera,of
Your smile
eyes knees and of your Etcetera)

Vera Brittain

Vera Brittain was born in 1893. In 1914 she won a place to study English Literature at Somerville College Oxford, despite resistance from her parents. At the end of her first year she suspended her studies to train as a VAD nurse. In 1916 she was sent to Malta and then asked for transfer to France, where her experience of nursing German prisoners had a profound impact on her thinking about the war.

Verses of a V.A.D. was published in 1918 and the following year she resumed her studies at Oxford, switching to Modern History which she thought might help her to understand 'how the whole calamity [of the war] had happened, to know why it had been possible for me and my contemporaries, through our own ignorance and others' ingenuity, to be used, hypnotised and slaughtered.'

Brittain became a prolific and successful journalist and writer, as well as a high-profile campaigner for peace, nuclear disarmament and women's rights. Her first novel, *The Dark Tide,* was published in 1923. Critical recognition and popularity came with *Testament of Youth: an Autobiographical Study of the Years 1900 – 1925.* Other books include *Honourable Estate: a Novel of Transition* (1936) and *Testament of Friendship: the Story of Winifred Holtby* (1940).

A Military Hospital

A mass of human wreckage, drifting in
  Borne on a blood-red tide,
Some never more to brave the stormy sea
  Laid reverently aside,
And some with love restored to sail again
  For regions far and wide.

The Troop Train

(France, 1917)
As we came down from Amiens,
  And they went up the line,
They waved their careless hands to us,
  And cheered the Red Cross sign.

And often I have wondered since,
  Repicturing that train,
How many of those laughing souls
  Came down the line again.

The German Ward

('Inter arma caritas')

When the years of strife are over and my recollection
       fades
  Of the wards wherein I worked the weeks away,
I shall still see, as a vision rising 'mid the War-time
       shades,
  The ward in France where German wounded lay.

I shall see the pallid faces and the half-suspicious eyes,
  I shall hear the bitter groans and laboured breath,
And recall the loud complaining and the weary tedious
      cries,
  And sights and smells of blood and wounds and death.

I shall see the convoy cases, blanket-covered on the
      floor,
  And watch the heavy stretcher-work begin,
And the gleam of knives and bottles through the open
      theatre door,
  And the operation patients carried in.

I shall see the Sister standing, with her form of
      youthful grace,
  And the humour and the wisdom of her smile,
And the tale of three years' warfare on her thin
      expressive face —
  The weariness of many a toil-filled while.

I shall think of how I worked for her with nerve and
      heart and mind,
  And marvelled at her courage and her skill,

And how the dying enemy her tenderness would find
  Beneath her scornful energy of will.

And I learnt that human mercy turns alike to friend or
      foe
  When the darkest hour of all is creeping nigh,
And those who slew our dearest, when their lamps
      were burning low,
  Found help and pity ere they came to die.

So, though much will be forgotten when the sound of
      War's alarms
  And the days of death and strife have passed away,
I shall always see the vision of Love working amidst
      arms
  In the ward wherein the wounded prisoners lay.

War

(The great German Offensive, March-May 1918)
A night of storm and thunder crashing by,
  A bitter night of tempest and of rain–
Then calm at dawn beneath a wind-swept sky,
  And broken flowers that will not bloom again.

An age of Death and Agony and Tears,
  A cruel age of woe unguessed before–
Then peace to close the weary storm-wrecked years,
  And broken hearts that bleed for evermore.

'Vengeance is Mine'

(In memory of the Sisters who died in the Great Air Raid upon hospitals at Étaples)

Who shall avenge us for anguish unnamable,
  Rivers of scarlet and crosses of grey,
Terror of night-time and blood-lust untamable,
  Hate without pity where broken we lay?

How could we help them, in agony calling us,
  Those whom we laboured to comfort and save,
How still their moaning, whose hour was befalling us,
  Crushed in a horror more dark than the grave?

Burning of canvas and smashing of wood above–
  Havoc of Mercy's toil – shall He forget
Us that have fallen, Who numbers in gracious love
  Each tiny creature whose life is man's debt?

Will He not hear us, though speech is now failing us–
  Voices too feeble to utter a cry?
Shall they not answer, the foemen assailing us,
  Women who suffer and women who die?

Who shall avenge us for anguish unnamable,
  Rivers of scarlet and crosses of grey,
Terror of night-time and blood-lust untamable,
  Hate without pity where broken we lay?

Epitaph on My Days in Hospital

I found in you a holy place apart,
Sublime endurance, God in man revealed,
Where mending broken bodies slowly healed
My broken heart.

The Lament of the Demobilised

'Four years,' some say consolingly,
        'Oh well,
What's that? You're young. And then it must have been
A very fine experience for you!'
And they forget
How others stayed behind and just got on–
Got on the better since we were away.
And we came home and found
They had achieved, and men revered their names,
But never mentioned ours;
And no one talked heroics now, and we
Must just go back and start again once more.
'You threw four years into the melting-pot–
Did you indeed!' these others cry.
        'Oh well,
The more fool you!'
And we're beginning to agree with them.

Mary Borden

Mary Borden was born in Chicago in 1886. The death of her prospector father left her independently wealthy at an early age. By 1914 she was married with three small children and living in London. She joined the Suffragette movement and was briefly imprisoned after throwing a stone through a window of the Treasury during a demonstration in Parliament Square. At the outbreak of war she used her money to establish a field hospital for the French Army based close to the fighting on the Somme. The hospital, which she ran personally, treated 25,000 soldiers in its first six weeks.

While serving at the Front she began an affair with Louis Spears, then a young liaison officer working with the British and French high commands. She married him in 1918.

In 1929 she published *The Forbidden Zone*, a remarkable account of her war experience told in poetry and prose. This was followed by many successful novels including *Jane Our Stranger* and *Sarah Gay*.

During the Second World War she ran a mobile ambulance unit which saw active service in France and the Middle East. She described this in *Journey Down a Blind Alley* (1946).

A number of her poems, including the sonnets for Louis Spears and 'Come to me quickly', were not published in her lifetime, and were found as handwritten drafts among her papers.

The Song of the Mud

This is the song of the mud,
The pale yellow glistening mud that covers the hills
      like satin;
The grey gleaming silvery mud that is spread like
      enamel over the valleys;
The frothing, squirting, spurting, liquid mud that
      gurgles along the road beds;
The thick elastic mud that is kneaded and pounded
      and squeezed under the hoofs of the horses;
The invincible, inexhaustible mud of the war zone.

This is the song of the mud, the uniform of the poilu.
His coat is of mud, his great dragging flapping coat,
      that is too big for him and too heavy;
His coat that once was blue and now is grey and stiff
      with the mud that cakes to it.
This is the mud that clothes him.
His trousers and boots are of mud,
And his skin is of mud;
And there is mud in his beard.
His head is crowned with a helmet of mud.
He wears it well.
He wears it as a king wears the ermine that bores him.
He has set a new style in clothing;
He has introduced the chic of mud.

This is the song of the mud that wriggles its way into
      battle.
The impertinent, the intrusive, the ubiquitous, the
      unwelcome,
The slimy inveterate nuisance,

That fills the trenches,
That mixes in with the food of the soldiers,
That spoils the working of motors and crawls into their
     secret parts,
That spreads itself over the guns,
That sucks the guns down and holds them fast in its
     slimy voluminous lips,
That has no respect for destruction and muzzles the
     bursting shells;
And slowly, softly, easily,
Soaks up the fire, the noise; soaks up the energy and
     the courage;
Soaks up the power of armies;
Soaks up the battle.
Just soaks it up and thus stops it.

This is the hymn of mud – the obscene, the filthy, the
     putrid,
The vast liquid grave of our armies.
It has drowned our men.
Its monstrous distended belly reeks with the undigested
     dead.
Our men have gone into it, sinking slowly, and struggling
     and slowly disappearing.
Our fine men, our brave, strong, young men;
Our glowing red, shouting, brawny men.
Slowly, inch by inch, they have gone down into it,
Into its darkness, its thickness, its silence.
Slowly, irresistibly, it drew them down, sucked them down,
And they were drowned in thick, bitter, heaving mud.
Now it hides them, Oh, so many of them!
Under its smooth glistening surface it is hiding them
     blandly.

There is not a trace of them.
There is no mark where they went down.
The mute enormous mouth of the mud has closed
       over them.

This is the song of the mud,
The beautiful glistening golden mud that covers the
       hills like satin;
The mysterious gleaming silvery mud that is spread like
       enamel over the valleys.
Mud, the disguise of the war zone;
Mud, the mantle of battles;
Mud, the smooth fluid grave of our soldiers:
This is the song of the mud.

Unidentified

Look well at this man. Look!
Come up out of your graves, philosophers,
And you who founded churches, and all you
Who for ten thousand years have talked of God.
Come out of your uncomfortable tombs, astronomers,
Who raked the heavens with your mighty eyes,
And died, unanswered questions on your lips,
For you have something interesting to learn
By looking at this man.

Stand all about, you many-legioned ghosts;
Fill up the desert with your shadowy forms,
And in the vast resounding waste of death,
Watch him while he dies;
He will not notice you.

Observe his ugliness.
See how he stands there planted in the mud like some
old battered image of a faith forgotten by its God.
Note his naked neck and jutting jaw under the iron hat
          that's jammed upon his head;
See how he rounds his shoulders, bends his back inside
          his clumsy coat;
And how he leans ahead, gripping with grimy fists
The muzzle of his gun that digs it butt-end down into
          the mud between the solid columns of his legs.

Look close, come close, pale ghosts!
Come back out of the dim unfinished past;
Crowd up across the edges of the earth,
Where the horizon, like a red hot wire, twists

underneath tremendous smoking blows.

Come up, come up across the quaking ground that
gapes in sudden holes beneath your feet;

Come fearlessly across the twisting field where bones
of men stick through the tortured mud.

Ghosts have no need to fear.

Look close at this man. Look!

He waits for death;

He watches it approach;

His little bloodshot eyes can see it bearing down on
every side;

He feels it coming underneath his feet, running,
burrowing underneath the ground;

He hears it screaming in the frantic air.

Death that tears the shrieking sky in two,

That suddenly explodes out of the festering bowels of
the earth –

Dreadful and horrid death.

He takes the impact of it on his back, his back, his chest,
his belly and his arms;

Spreads his legs upon its lurching form;

Plants his feet upon its face and breathes deep into his
pumping lungs the gassy breath of death.

He does not move.

In all the running landscape there's a solitary thing
that's motionless:

The figure of this man.

The sky long since has fallen from its dome.

Terror let loose like a gigantic wind has torn it from
the ceiling of the world,

And it is flapping down in frantic shreds.

The earth ages ago leaped screaming up out of the

fastness of its ancient laws.
There is no centre now to hold it down.
It rolls and writhes, a shifting tortured thing, a floating
       mass of matter set adrift.
And in between the fluttering tatters of the ruined sky,
And the convulsions of the maddened earth,
The man stands solid.
Something holds him there.

What holds him, timid ghosts?
What do you say, you shocked and shuddering ghosts,
Dragged from your sheltered vaults;
You who once died in quiet lamp-lit rooms;
Who were companioned to the end by friends;
And closed your eyes in languor on a world
That you had fashioned for your pleasant selves?
You scorned this man.
He was for you an ordinary man.
Some of you pitied him, prayed over his soul, worried
       him with stories of Heaven and Hell.
Promised him Heaven if he would be ashamed of being
       what he was,
And everlasting sorrow if he died as he had lived, an
       ordinary man.
You gave him Gods he could not know, and images of
       God; laws he could not keep, and punishment.
You were afraid of him.
Everything about him that was his very own
Made you afraid of him.
His love of women, food and drink, and fun,
His clumsy reach for life, his open grabbing fist,
His stupid open gaping heart and mouth.
He was a hungry man,

And you were afraid of him.
None of you trusted him;
No one of you was his friend.

Look at him now. Look well, look long.
Your hungry brute, your ordinary man;
Your fornicator, drunkard, anarchist;
Your ruthless rough seed-sowing male;
Your angry greedy egotist;
Your lost, bewildered, childish dunce;
Come close and look into his haggard face.
It is too late to do him justice now, or even speak to him.
But look.
Look at the stillness of his face.
It's made of little fragile bones and flesh, tissued of
        quivering muscles fine as silk;
Exquisite nerves, soft membrane warm with blood,
That travels smoothly through the tender veins.
One blow, one minute more, and that man's face will
        be a mass of matter, horrid slime and little brittle
        splinters.
He knows.
He waits.
His face remains quite still.
And underneath the bullet-spattered helmet on his head
His steady eyes look out.
What is it that looks out?
What is deep mirrored in those bloodshot eyes?
Terror? No.
Despair? Perhaps.
What else?
Ah, poor ghosts – poor blind unseeing ghosts!
It is his self you see;

His self that does remember what he loved and what
      he wanted, and what he never had;
His self that can regret, that can reproach its own self
      now; his self that gave itself, let loose its hold of
      all but just itself.

Is that, then, nothing? Just his naked self, pinning down
      a shaking world,
A single rivet driven down to hold a universe together.

Go back, poor ghosts. Go back into your graves.
He has no use for you, this nameless man.
Scholars, philosophers, men of God, leave this man alone.
No lamp you lit will show his soul the way;
No name restore his lost identity.
The guns will chant his death march down the world;
The flare of cannon light his dying;
The mute and nameless men beneath his feet will
welcome him beside them in the mud.
Take one last look and leave him standing there,
Unfriended, unrewarded, and unknown.

Come to me quickly and take me away

Come to me quickly and take me away from my
      wounded men –
I cannot bear their pain anymore –
Come quickly and take me away out of this place
Give me rest, give me strength, give me cleanness and
      joy for one hour.
I am suffocating –
I cannot get away –
They cling to my skirts, my arms
My hands –
They clutch at my strength
They call my name – They keep calling me.
They cry to me to undo their pain and let them free –
I cannot set them free.
They throw themselves onto my breast, to die –
I cannot even let them die –
Come to me for one hour, strong, clean – whole –
Their wounds gape at me –
Their stumps menace me –
Their bandaged faces grimace at me
Their death rattle curses me –
Give me rest – Make me clean

I am stained – I am soiled –
I am streaked with their blood –
I am soaked with the odor of the oozing of their
      wounds –
I am saturated with the poison of their poor festering
      wounds –
I am poisoned – I'm infected – I shall never wash it off –
But you are clean –

Your face is cold and fresh and wet by the rain –
Let me drink the fresh moisture of your face with my
    lips –
Your garments are electric with the wild blowing wind –
Put your gallant cloak about me –
Let me breathe, Let me breathe –
Give me rest –
Take me in your arms, your strong accustomed arms
    and swing me up and hold me close
and quietly oh quietly set me afloat upon your
    tenderness
That I may be light – light –
For I am heavy with the weight of my helpless wounded
    men –
I can bear no more the weight of their rolling heads,
their broken limbs, their inert bodies.
Give me strength –
Stop the shaking of my hands –
I am shaking – I cannot keep from shaking
I am shaking because I have had to be strong for so long.
When they clung to me I held them –
When they tossed I held them still –
When they fought I held them down –
When they clutched at me, sinking, drowning in their
    agony, I held them.
Oh how I tried to hold them up and save them.
But their pain was so strong that it has left me shaking.
I can't hold them any more –
Give me strength –
And give me joy –
I emplore you – I beseech you – Give me joy for one
    hour –
That I may go back again to comfort them.

Take me out through the dark and up the hill
Where the wind and the roar of cannon surge and beat
      about us –
Where the flares run red through the wide luminous
      blackness –
There speak to me quietly – you who have never failed
      me –
Say my name with confidence
Repeat my name to me –
The sound of your voice saying my name
Assures me that I have always sufficed you.
Listen – I hear their delirium calling.
Speak to me quietly –
Let the war thunder –
Tell me that in our house the chimney fires are burning –
The quiet rooms are waiting.
And the tall trees are protecting the place that we have
      left, the place where we will go, again, someday.
Hold me still and let me listen to the faint far echoing
      music of the youth we had together –
Hold me and let me hear the chanting of the years, all
      the years that you have loved me,
the sure deep splendid years, with you who never failed
      me –
Ah, you who have always loved me,
Come to me for an hour
Then let me go back to my wounded men

What more can the desolate murmuring sea

What more can the desolate murmuring sea
Say to my heart, since you have kissed my lips?
What terror does it hold, what mystery
That I ignore? Those far white phantom ships
Riding the dim horizon to the south
Travel no farther than my fearful soul
Each night that I lie clinging to your mouth –
Then in your arms I cross from pole to pole
The sobbing waste, I visit the pale moon
And learn the hopeless passion of the tide.
Dive down to guilty caverns, in a swoon
Drift up again and of a sudden ride
Stupendous storms until at last I lie
Dying upon your heart and glad to die –

No, no! There is some sinister mistake

No, no! There is some sinister mistake.
You cannot love me now. I am no more
A thing to touch, a pleasant thing to take
Into one's arms. How can a man adore
A woman with black blood upon her face,
A cap of horror on her pallid head,
Mirrors of madness in the sunken place
Of eyes; hands dripping with the slimy dead?
Go. Cover close your proud untainted brow.
Go quickly. Leave me to the hungry lust
Of monstrous pain. I am his mistress now –
These are the frantic beds of his delight –
Here I succumb to him, anew, each night.

See how the withered leaves

See how the withered leaves lie shivering
Along the gutters of the autumn street.
They are the souls of women; quivering
Shrivelled souls of women who once were sweet
To the desiring lips of hungry men.
Now they adorn the road where pleasure rides
Poor withered things –Yes, kiss me once again
Who knows what bitterness the future hides?
Kiss me until you've kissed my mouth away
Wear out my flesh with your enamoured hands
Drink up my heart beats, one by one and say
That I have satisfied your fierce demands –
Ah look, the frightened leaves are fluttering
Before the wind, the wind that's muttering.

Geoffrey Studdert Kennedy

Geoffrey Studdert Kennedy was born in Leeds in 1883. After studying Classics and Divinity at Trinity College Dublin he was ordained in the Church of England. In 1915 he volunteered as an army chaplain and began a famous ministry to soldiers serving on the Western Front, where he also volunteered as a stretcher-bearer and medical aide. He was a popular figure among the troops who responded to his easy-going humour and warmth, as well as his personal honesty and bravery. He was awarded the Military Cross for helping the wounded while under fire. He described his own approach to chaplaincy as needing 'a box of fags in your haversack, and a great deal of love in your heart'.

Behind the jokes and the popular Kiplingesque rhymes was a serious figure who challenged established theological and political orthodoxy. After the war he became a chaplain to the King and an outspoken champion of the working poor. His books and public talks commanded large audiences. The Archbishop of Canterbury William Temple described him as 'the finest priest I have known'.

Woodbine Willie

They gave me this name like their nature,
Compacted of laughter and tears,
A sweet that was born of the bitter,
A joke that was torn from the years

Of their travail and torture, Christ's fools,
Atoning my sins with their blood,
Who grinned in their agony sharing
The glorious madness of God.

Their name! Let me hear it – the symbol
Of unpaid – unpayable debt,
For the men to whom I owed God's Peace,
I put off with a cigarette.

Her Gift

Dead black against a blood-red sky
      It stands,
With outstretched hands,
      The Calvary.
What can it mean,
Beyond the vain recalling of a scene,
A shameful scene of centuries ago?
And yet, if that be so,
      How can it be,
      For you and me,
A thing of any worth at all?
We've seen men die,
Not once, nor twice, but many times
      In agony
As ghastly to behold as that.
We've seen men fall,
And rise, and staggering onward fall again,
Bedrenched in their own blood,
Fast flowing like a flood,
Of crimson sacrifice upon the snow.
We've seen, and would forget.
Why then should there be set
Before our eyes these monuments of crime?
It's time, high time,
That they were buried in the past;
There let them lie,
In that great sea of merciful oblivion,
      Where our vile deeds,
      And outworn creeds,
      Are left to rot and die.
      We would forget,

And yet,
Do you remember Rob McNeil
    And how he died,
    And cried,
And pleaded with his men
    To take that gun,
    And kill the Hun
    That worked it, dead?
    He bled
Horribly. Do you remember?
I can't forget,
I would not if I could,
It were not right I should;
    He died for me.
He was a God, that boy,
The only God I could adore.
And that reminds me I have something here
He wore:
He gave it me that night,
But because my heart was sore
With grief, I have not dared to look at it.
But here it is, a little leather case,
A picture, maybe, of the face
That smiled upon him as a babe,
    All wondering bright,
    With mother light,
Of tenderest pride and love.
The face that oft would dimple into laughter
At his first baby tricks.
It is her gift: but look at it–
    A little silver Crucifix.

Waste

Waste of Muscle, waste of Brain,
Waste of Patience, waste of Pain,
Waste of Manhood, waste of Health,
Waste of Beauty, waste of Wealth,
Waste of Blood, and waste of Tears,
Waste of Youth's most precious years,
Waste of ways the Saints have trod,
Waste of Glory, waste of God,–
War!

Solomon in All His Glory

Still I see them coming, coming
  In their ragged broken line,
Walking wounded in the sunlight,
  Clothed in majesty divine.

For the fairest of the lilies,
  That God's summer ever sees,
Ne'er was clothed in royal beauty
  Such as decks the least of these.

Tattered, torn, and bloody khaki,
  Gleams of white flesh in the sun,
Raiment worthy of their beauty
  And the great things they have done.

Purple robes and snowy linen
  Have for earthly kings sufficed,
But these bloody sweaty tatters
  Were the robes of Jesus Christ.

His Mate

There's a broken, battered village
　Somewhere up behind the line,
There's a dug-out and a bunk there,
　That I used to say were mine.

I remember how I reached them,
　Dripping wet and all forlorn,
In the dim and dreary twilight
　Of a weeping summer morn.

All that week I'd buried brothers,
　In one bitter battle slain,
In one grave I laid two hundred.
　God! What sorrow and what rain!

And that night I'd been in trenches,
　Seeking out the sodden dead,
And just dropping them in shell-holes,
　With a service swiftly said.

For the bullets rattled round me,
　But I couldn't leave them there,
Water-soaked in flooded shell-holes,
　Reft of common Christian prayer.

So I crawled round on my belly,
　And I listened to the roar
Of the guns that hammered Thiepval,
　Like big breakers on the shore.

Then there spoke a dripping sergeant,

When the time was growing late,
"Would you please to bury this one,
  'Cause 'e used to be my mate?"

So we groped our way in darkness
  To a body lying there,
Just a blacker lump of blackness,
  With a red blotch on his hair.

Though we turned him gently over,
  Yet I still can hear the thud,
As the body fell face forward,
  And then settled in the mud.

We went down upon our faces,
  And I said the service through,
From "I am the Resurrection,"
  To the last, the great "adieu."

We stood up to give the Blessing,
  And commend him to the Lord,
When a sudden light shot soaring
  Silver swift and like a sword.

At a stroke it slew the darkness,
  Flashed its glory on the mud,
And I saw the sergeant staring
  At a crimson clot of blood.

There are many kinds of sorrow
  In this world of Love and Hate,
But there is no sterner sorrow
  Than a soldier's for his mate.

Dead and Buried

I have borne my cross through Flanders,
  Through the broken heart of France,
I have borne it through the deserts of the East;
  I have wandered, faint and longing,
  Through the human hosts that, thronging,
Swarmed to glut their grinning idols with a feast.

  I was crucified in Cambrai,
  And again outside Bapaume;
I was scourged for miles along the Albert Road,
  I was driven, pierced and bleeding,
  With a million maggots feeding
On the body that I carried as my load.

I have craved a cup of water,
  Just a drop to quench my thirst,
As the routed armies ran to keep the pace;
  But no soldier made reply
  As the maddened hosts swept by,
And a sweating straggler kicked me in the face.

  There's no ecstasy of torture
  That the devils e'er devised,
That my soul has not endured unto the last;
  As I bore my cross of sorrow,
  For the glory of to-morrow,
Through the wilderness of battles that is past.

  Yet my heart was still unbroken,
  And my hope was still unquenched,
Till I bore my cross to Paris through the crowd.

Soldiers pierced me on the Aisne,
But 'twas by the river Seine
That the statesmen brake my legs and made my shroud.

There they wrapped my mangled body
In fine linen of fair words,
With the perfume of a sweetly scented lie,
And they laid it in the tomb
Of the golden-mirrored room,
'Mid the many-fountained Garden of Versailles.

With a thousand scraps of paper
They made fast the open door,
And the wise men of the Council saw it sealed.
With the seal of subtle lying
They made certain of my dying,
Lest the torment of the peoples should be healed.

Then they set a guard of soldiers
Night and day beside the Tomb,
Where the Body of the Prince of Peace is laid,
And the captains of the nations
Keep the sentries to their stations,
Lest the statesman's trust from Satan be betrayed.

For it isn't steel and iron
That men use to kill their God,
But the poison of a smooth and slimy tongue.
Steel and iron tear the body,
But it's oily sham and shoddy
That have trampled down God's *Spirit* in the dung.

To Stretcher-Bearers

Easy does it – bit o' trench 'ere,
Mind that blinkin' bit o' wire,
There's a shell 'ole on your left there,
Lift 'im up a little 'igher.
Stick it, lad, ye'll soon be there now,
Want to rest 'ere for a while?
Let 'im dahn then – gently – gently,
There ye are, lad. That's the style.
Want a drink, mate? 'Ere's my bottle,
Lift 'is 'ead up for 'im, Jack,
Put my tunic underneath 'im,
'Ow's that, chummy ? That's the tack!
Guess we'd better make a start now,
Ready for another spell?
Best be goin', we won't 'urt ye,
But 'e might just start to shell.
Are ye right, mate? Off we goes then.
That's well over on the right;
Gawd Almighty, that's a near 'un!
'Old your end up good and tight,
Never mind, lad, you're for Blighty.
Mind this rotten bit o' board.

We'll soon 'ave ye tucked in bed, lad,
'Opes ye gets to my old ward.
No more war for you, my 'earty,
This'll get ye well away,
Twelve good months in dear old Blighty,
Twelve good months if you're a day.
M.O.'s got a bit o' something
What'll stop that blarsted pain.

'Ere's a rotten bit o' ground, mate,
Lift up 'igher – up again,
Wish 'e'd stop 'is blarsted shellin',
Makes it rotten for the lad.
When a feller's been and got it,
It affec's 'im twice as bad.
'Ow's it goin' now then, sonny?
'Ere's that narrow bit o' trench,
Careful, mate, there's some dead Jerries.
Gawd Almighty, what a stench!
'Ere we are now, stretcher-case, boys,
Bring him aht a cup o' tea!
Inasmuch as ye have done it
Ye have done it unto Me.

John Masefield

John Masefield was born in Ledbury in1878. He trained as a merchant navy officer and aged sixteen sailed for Chile on the four-masted iron sailing ship *Gilcruix*. On a later voyage he jumped ship in New York and led a restless life travelling across America and working in bars in Greenwich Village. He drew on his experiences at sea to write poetry that attracted a wide and appreciative audience. *Salt-Water Ballads* (1902) included 'Sea-fever' and 'Cargoes' which have proved enduringly popular.

When war broke out Masefield joined the French Red Cross and served first as a medical orderly at Arc-en-Barrois. On later visits to France he drove an ambulance and toured the Somme battlefields. He raised significant funds for the Red Cross which enabled the provision of five ambulance motor boats at Gallipoli, one of which he personally commanded.

Masefield was commissioned by the Government to write accounts of the Gallipoli campaign and the Battle of the Somme. He also gave a celebrated lecture tour in the USA to promote the British war effort.

Masefield was appointed Poet Laureate in 1930, by which time he was established as a popular and successful poet and novelist who also wrote books for children, including *The Midnight Folk* (1927) and *The Box of Delights* (1935).

August, 1914

How still this quiet cornfield is to-night!
By an intenser glow the evening falls,
Bringing, not darkness, but a deeper light;
Among the stooks a partridge covey calls.

The windows glitter on the distant hill;
Beyond the hedge the sheep-bells in the fold
Stumble on sudden music and are still;
The forlorn pinewoods droop above the wold.

An endless quiet valley reaches out
Past the blue hills into the evening sky;
Over the stubble, cawing, goes a rout
Of rooks from harvest, flagging as they fly.

So beautiful it is, I never saw
So great a beauty on these English fields,
Touched by the twilight's coming into awe,
Ripe to the soul and rich with summer's yields.

     *   *   *   *   *

These homes, this valley spread below me here,
The rooks, the tilted stacks, the beasts in pen,
Have been the heartfelt things, past-speaking dear
To unknown generations of dead men,

Who, century after century, held these farms,
And, looking out to watch the changing sky,
Heard, as we hear, the rumours and alarms
Of war at hand and danger pressing nigh.

And knew, as we know, that the message meant

The breaking off of ties, the loss of friends,
Death, like a miser getting in his rent,
And no new stones laid where the trackway ends.

The harvest not yet won, the empty bin,
The friendly horses taken from the stalls,
The fallow on the hill not yet brought in,
The cracks unplastered in the leaking walls.

Yet heard the news, and went discouraged home,
And brooded by the fire with heavy mind,
With such dumb loving of the Berkshire loam
As breaks the dumb hearts of the English kind,

Then sadly rose and left the well-loved Downs,
And so by ship to sea, and knew no more
The fields of home, the byres, the market towns,
Nor the dear outline of the English shore,

But knew the misery of the soaking trench,
The freezing in the rigging, the despair
In the revolting second of the wrench
When the blind soul is flung upon the air,

And died (uncouthly, most) in foreign lands
For some idea but dimly understood
Of an English city never built by hands
Which love of England prompted and made good.

     *   *   *   *   *

If there be any life beyond the grave,
It must be near the men and things we love,
Some power of quick suggestion how to save,
Touching the living soul as from above.

An influence from the Earth from those dead hearts
So passionate once, so deep, so truly kind,
That in the living child the spirit starts,
Feeling companioned still, not left behind.

Surely above these fields a spirit broods
A sense of many watchers muttering near
Of the lone Downland with the forlorn woods
Loved to the death, inestimably dear.

A muttering from beyond the veils of Death
From long-dead men, to whom this quiet scene
Came among blinding tears with the last breath,
The dying soldier's vision of his queen.

All the unspoken worship of those lives
Spent in forgotten wars at other calls
Glimmers upon these fields where evening drives
Beauty like breath, so gently darkness falls.

Darkness that makes the meadows holier still,
The elm-trees sadden in the hedge, a sigh
Moves in the beech-clump on the haunted hill,
The rising planets deepen in the sky,

And silence broods like spirit on the brae,
A glimmering moon begins, the moonlight runs
Over the grasses of the ancient way
Rutted this morning by the passing guns.

Here, where we stood together

Here, where we stood together, we three men,
Before the war had swept us to the East
Three thousand miles away, I stand again
And hear the bells, and breathe, and go to feast.
We trod the same path, to the self-same place,
Yet here I stand, having beheld their graves,
Skyros whose shadows the great seas erase,
And Seddul Bahr that ever more blood craves.
So, since we communed here, our bones have been
Nearer, perhaps, than they again will be,
Earth and the worldwide battle lie between,
Death lies between, and friend-destroying sea.
Yet here, a year ago, we talked and stood
As I stand now, with pulses beating blood.

I saw her like a shadow on the sky

I saw her like a shadow on the sky
In the last light, a blur upon the sea,
Then the gale's darkness put the shadow by,
But from one grave that island talked to me;
And, in the midnight, in the breaking storm,
I saw its blackness and a blinking light,
And thought, "So death obscures your gentle form,
So memory strives to make the darkness bright;
And, in that heap of rocks, your body lies,
Part of the island till the planet ends,
My gentle comrade, beautiful and wise,
Part of this crag this bitter surge offends,
While I, who pass, a little obscure thing,
War with this force, and breathe, and am its king."

Any Dead to Any Living

Boast not about our score.
Think this:– There was no need
For such a Sack of Youth
As burned our lives.
We, and the millions more,
Were Waste, from want of heed,
From world-wide hate of truth,
And souls in gyves.
Let the dead bury the dead.
Let the great graveyard be.
Life had not health to climb,
It loved no strength that saves.
Furbish our million graves
As records of a crime;
But give our brothers bread,
Unfetter heart and head,
Set prisoned angels free.

Red Cross

I remember a moonless night in a blasted town,
And the cellar-steps with their army-blanket-screen,
And the stretcher-bearers, groping and stumbling down
To the Red Cross struggle with Death in the ill-lit scene.

There, entering-in, I saw, at a table near,
A surgeon tense by a man who struggled for breath.
A shell, that shattered above us, rattled the gear,
The dying one looked at me, as if I were Death.

He died, and was borne away, and the surgeon wept;
An elderly man, well-used, as one would have thought
To western war and the revels that Death then kept:
Why weep for one when a million ranked as naught?

He said, 'We have buried heaps since the push began.
From now to the Peace we'll bury a thousand more.
It's silly to cry, but I could have saved that man
Had they only carried him in an hour before.'

Robert Service

Born in 1874, Robert Service grew up in Scotland. At the age of twenty-two he travelled extensively before settling in Canada where he began to write rhyming ballads and 'story poems' about the Klondike gold rush and the rough life of 'sourdoughs' (prospectors) in the northern wilderness. *Songs of a Sourdough* (1907, called *The Spell of the Yukon* in the US) and *Ballads of a Cheechako* (1909) captured the imagination of millions of readers. His wood cabin is now a visitor attraction.

When war broke out in 1914 he was over-age for military service. He visited the war zone as a freelance correspondent but was arrested on suspicion of spying. He then volunteered with an American ambulance unit, often choosing the most dangerous roles at forward first aid stations and carrying stretchers out of the firing trench and No Man's Land. Illness brought this work to an end, after which he toured France on behalf of Canadian Intelligence. His horror at the brutal scenes he witnessed led him to tear up his report.

His war experiences inspired a group of extremely popular poems and ballads that appeared in *Rhymes of a Red Cross Man* (1916), and *Ballads of a Bohemian* (1921), in which the poems were prefaced with short vivid prose accounts of his time at the front.

A Song of the Sandbags

No, Bill, I'm not a-spooning out no patriotic tosh
(The cove be'ind the sandbags ain't a death-or-glory cuss).
And though I strafes 'em good and 'ard I doesn't 'ate
    the Boche,
I guess they're mostly decent, just the same as most of us.
I guess they loves their 'omes and kids as much as you
    or me;
And just the same as you or me they'd rather shake
    than fight;
And if we'd 'appened to be born at Berlin-on-the-Spree,
We'd be out there with 'Ans and Fritz, dead sure that
    we was right.

      A-standin' up to the sandbags
      It's funny the thoughts wot come;
      Starin' into the darkness,
      'Earin' the bullets 'um;
      (*Zing! Zip! Ping! Rip!*
      'ark 'ow the bullets 'um!)
      A-leanin' against the sandbags
      Wiv me rifle under me ear,
      Oh, I've 'ad more thoughts on a sentry-go
      Than I used to 'ave in a year.

I wonder, Bill, if 'Ans and Fritz is wonderin' like me
Wot's at the bottom of it all? Wot all the slaughter's for?
'E thinks 'e's right (of course 'e ain't) but this we both
    agree,
If them as made it 'ad to fight, there wouldn't be no war.
If them as lies in feather beds while we kips in the mud;
If them as makes their fortoons while we fights for 'em

like 'ell;
If them as slings their pot of ink just 'ad to sling their
        blood:
By Crust! I'm thinkin' there 'ud be another tale to tell.

Shiverin' up to the sandbags,
With a hicicle 'stead of a spine,
Don't it seem funny the things you think
'Ere in the firin' line:
(*Whee! Whut! Ziz! Zut!*
Lord! 'ow the bullets whine!)
Hunkerin' down when a star-shell
Cracks in a sputter of light,
You can jaw to yer soul by the sandbags
Most any old time o' night.

They talks o' England's glory and a-'oldin' of our trade,
Of Empire and 'igh destiny until we're fair flim-flammed;
But if it's for the likes o' that that bloody war is made,
Then wot I say is: Empire and 'igh destiny be damned!
There's only one good cause, Bill, for poor blokes like
        us to fight:
That's self-defence, for 'earth and 'ome, and them that
        bears our name;
And that's wot I'm a-doin' by the sandbags 'ere tonight...
But Fritz out there will tell you 'e's a-doin' of the same.

Starin' over the sandbags,
Sick of the 'ole damn thing;
Firin' to keep meself awake,
'Earin' the bullets sing.
(*Hiss! Twang! Tsing! Pang!*
Saucy the bullets sing.)

Dreamin' 'ere by the sandbags
Of a day when war will cease,
When 'Ans and Fritz and Bill and me
Will clink our mugs in fraternity,
And the Brotherhood of Labour will be
The Brotherhood of Peace.

Only a Boche

We brought him in from between the lines: we'd better
    have let him lie;
For what's the use of risking one's skin for a *tyke* that's
    going to die?
What's the use of tearing him loose under a gruelling fire,
When he's shot in the head, and worse than dead, and
    all messed up on the wire?

However, I say, we brought him in. *Diable!* The mud
    was bad;
The trench was crooked and greasy and high, and oh,
    what a time we had!
And often we slipped, and often we tripped, but never
    he made a moan;
And how we were wet with blood and with sweat! but
    we carried him in like our own.

Now there he lies in the dug-out dim, awaiting the
    ambulance,
And the doctor shrugs his shoulders at him, and remarks,
    "He hasn't a chance."
And we squat and smoke at our game of bridge on the
    glistening, straw-packed floor,
And above our oaths we can hear his breath deep-
    drawn in a kind of snore.

For the dressing station is long and low, and the candles
    gutter dim,
And the mean light falls on the cold clay walls and our
    faces bristly and grim;
And we flap our cards on the lousy straw, and we laugh

and jibe as we play,
And you'd never know that the cursed foe was less
    than a mile away.
As we con our cards in the rancid gloom, oppressed by
    that snoring breath,
You'd never dream that our broad roof-beam was swept
    by the broom of death.

Heigh-ho! My turn for the dummy hand; I rise and I
    stretch a bit;
The fetid air is making me yawn, and my cigarette's unlit,
So I go to the nearest candle flame, and the man we
    brought is there,
And his face is white in the shabby light, and I stand at
    his feet and stare.
Stand for a while, and quietly stare: for strange though
    it seems to be,
The dying Boche on the stretcher there has a queer
    resemblance to me.

It gives one a kind of a turn, you know, to come on a
    thing like that.
It's just as if I were lying there, with a turban of blood
    for a hat,
Lying there in a coat grey-green instead of a coat grey-
    blue,
With one of my eyes all shot away, and my brain half
    tumbling through;
Lying there with a chest that heaves like a bellows up
    and down,
And a cheek as white as snow on a grave, and lips that
    are coffee brown.

And confound him, too! He wears, like me, on his
finger a wedding ring,
And around his neck, as around my own, by a greasy
bit of string,
A locket hangs with a woman's face, and I turn it about
to see:
Just as I thought... on the other side the faces of children
three;
Clustered together cherub-like, three little laughing girls,
With the usual tiny rosebud mouths and the usual
silken curls.
"Zut!" I say. "He has beaten me; for me, I have only two,"
And I push the locket beneath his shirt, feeling a little
blue.

Oh, it isn't cheerful to see a man, the marvellous work
of God,
Crushed in the mutilation mill, crushed to a smeary clod;
Oh, it isn't cheerful to hear him moan; but it isn't that
I mind,
It isn't the anguish that goes with him, it's the anguish
he leaves behind.
For his going opens a tragic door that gives on a world
of pain,
And the death he dies, those who live and love, will die
again and again.

So here I am at my cards once more, but it's kind of
spoiling my play,
Thinking of those three brats of his so many a mile away.
War is war, and he's only a Boche, and we all of us take
our chance;
But all the same I'll be mighty glad when I'm hearing

the ambulance.

One foe the less, but all the same I'm heartily glad I'm not
The man who gave him his broken head, the sniper who
       fired the shot.

No trumps you make it, I think you said? You'll pardon
       me if I err;
For a moment I thought of other things... *Mon Dieu!*
       Quelle vache de guerre.

The Stretcher-Bearer

My stretcher is one scarlet stain,
And as I tries to scrape it clean,
I tell you wot — I'm sick with pain
For all I've 'eard, for all I've seen;
Around me is the 'ellish night,
And as the war's red rim I trace,
I wonder if in 'Eaven's height,
Our God don't turn away 'Is Face.

      I don't care 'oose the Crime may be;
      I 'olds no brief for kin or clan;
      I 'ymns no 'ate: I only see
      As man destroys his brother man;
      I waves no flag: I only know,
      As 'ere beside the dead I wait,
      A million 'earts is weighed with woe,
      A million 'omes is desolate.

In drippin' darkness, far and near,
All night I've sought them woeful ones.
Dawn shudders up and still I 'ear
The crimson chorus of the guns.
Look! like a ball of blood the sun
'Angs o'er the scene of wrath and wrong....
"Quick! Stretcher-bearers on the run!"
O Prince of Peace! 'ow long, 'ow long?

A Casualty

That boy I took in the car last night,
With the body that awfully sagged away,
And the lips blood-crisped, and the eyes flame-bright,
And the poor hands folded and cold as clay –
Oh, I've thought and I've thought of him all the day.

For the weary old doctor says to me:
"He'll only last for an hour or so.
Both of his legs below the knee
Blown off by a bomb… So, lad, go slow,
And please remember, he doesn't know."

So I tried to drive with never a jar;
And there was I cursing the road like mad,
When I hears a ghost of a voice from the car:
"Tell me, old chap, have I 'copped it' bad?"
So I answers "No," and he says, "I'm glad."

"Glad," says he, "for at twenty-two
Life's so splendid, I hate to go.
There's so much good that a chap might do,
And I've fought from the start and I've suffered so.
'Twould be hard to get knocked out now, you know."

"Forget it," says I; then I drove awhile,
And I passed him a cheery word or two;
But he didn't answer for many a mile,
So just as the hospital hove in view,
Says I: "Is there nothing that I can do?"

Then he opens his eyes and he smiles at me;

And he takes my hand in his trembling hold;
"Thank you – you're far too kind," says he:
"I'm awfully comfy – stay… let's see:
I fancy my blanket's come unrolled –
My *feet*, please wrap 'em – they're cold… they're cold."

Enemy Conscript

What are we fighting for,
We fellows who go to war?
fighting for Freedom's sake!
(You give me the belly-ache.)
Freedom to starve or slave!
Freedom! aye, in the grave.
Fighting for "hearth and home,"
Who haven't an inch of loam?
Hearth? Why even a byre
Can only be ours for hire.
Dying for future peace?
Killing that killing cease?
To hell with such tripe, I say.
"Sufficient unto the day."

It isn't much fun being dead.
Better to lie in bed,
Cuddle up to the wife,
Making, not taking life.
To the corpse that stinks in the clay,
Does it matter who wins the day?
What odds if tyrants reign?
They can't put irons on the brain.
One always can eat one's grub,
Smoke and drink in a pub.
There's happiness in a glass,
A pipe and the kiss of a lass.
It's the best we get anyhow,
In the life we are living now.

Who's wanting a hero's fate?

To the dead cheers come too late.
Flesh is softer than steel;
Wounds are weary to heal.
In the maniac hell of the fray
Who is there dares to say?
"Hate will be vanquished by Love;
God's in His Heaven above."

When those who govern us lead
The lads they command to bleed;
When rulers march at the head,
And statesmen fall with the dead;
When Kings leap into the fray,
Fight in the old-time way,
Perish beside their men,
Maybe, O maybe then
War will be part of the past,
Peace will triumph at last.

Meantime such lads as I,
Who wouldn't have harmed a fly,
Have got to get out and kill
Lads whom we bear no ill;
As simple as we, no doubt,
Who seek what it's all about;
Who die in defence of – what?
Homes that they haven't got;
Who perish when all they ask
is to finish the daily task;
Make bread for the little ones,
Not feed the greed of the guns,
When fields of battle are red,
And diplomats die in bed.

Laurence Binyon

Laurence Binyon was born in 1869. After studying at Oxford he joined the British Museum where he was to work for the next forty years, latterly as Keeper of Prints and Drawings. He was a distinguished art historian with particular expertise in Chinese and Japanese art. When war broke out in 1914 he was over-age for military service but wanted to be 'made use of' in some way. He took leave of absence to volunteer as a medical orderly at the 'English hospital' for French soldiers at Arc-en-Barrois near Verdun. In 1918 he wrote a detailed account of his own experiences and the wider activities of the Red Cross in France, re-issued in 2018 as *The Call and the Answer.*

Binyon is best known for writing the four lines of poetry that appear on thousands of war memorials and that are still read at every Service of Remembrance ('They shall grow not old as we that are left grow old…'). His best poetry, however, is more personal and was written in his later years. 'The Burning of the Leaves', a long poem about the Blitz in London written in 1942, is widely regarded as his masterpiece.

The Healers

In a vision of the night I saw them,
In the battles of the night.
'Mid the roar and the reeling shadows of blood
They were moving like light,

Light of the reason, guarded
Tense within the will,
As a lantern under a tossing of boughs
Burns steady and still.

With scrutiny calm, and with fingers
Patient as swift
They bind up the hurts and the pain-writhen
Bodies uplift,

Untired and defenceless; around them
With shrieks in its breath
Bursts stark from the terrible horizon
Impersonal death;

But they take not their courage from anger
That blinds the hot being;
They take not their pity from weakness;
Tender, yet seeing;

Feeling, yet nerved to the uttermost;
Keen, like steel;
Yet the wounds of the mind they are stricken with,
Who shall heal?

They endure to have eyes of the watcher

In hell, and not swerve
For an hour from the faith that they follow,
The light that they serve.

Man true to man, to his kindness
That overflows all,
To his spirit erect in the thunder
When all his forts fall, –

This light, in the tiger-mad welter
They serve and they save.
What song shall be worthy to sing of them –
Braver than the brave?

Fetching the Wounded

At the road's end glimmer the station lights;
How small beneath the immense hollow of Night's
Lonely and living silence! Air that raced
And tingled on the eyelids as we faced
The long road stretched between the poplars flying
To the dark behind us, shuddering and sighing
With phantom foliage, lapses into hush.
Magical supersession! The loud rush
Swims into quiet: midnight reassumes
Its solitude; there's nothing but great glooms,
Blurred stars; whispering gusts; the hum of wires.
And swerving leftwards upon noiseless tires
We glide over the grass that smells of dew.
A wave of wonder bathes my body through!
For there in the headlamps' gloom-surrounded beam
Tall flowers spring before us, like a dream,
Each luminous little green leaf intimate
And motionless, distinct and delicate
With powdery white bloom fresh upon the stem,
As if that clear beam had created them
Out of the darkness. Never so intense
I felt the pang of beauty's innocence,
Earthly and yet unearthly.

      A sudden call!
We leap to ground, and I forget it all.
Each hurries on his errand; lanterns swing;
Dark shapes cross and re-cross the rails; we bring
Stretchers, and pile and number them; and heap
The blankets ready. Then we wait and keep
A listening ear. Nothing comes yet; all's still.

Only soft gusts upon the wires blow shrill
Fitfully, with a gentle spot of rain.
Then, ere one knows it, the long gradual train
Creeps quietly in and slowly stops. No sound
But a few voices' interchange. Around
Is the immense night-stillness, the expanse
Of faint stars over all the wounds of France.

Now stale odour of blood mingles with keen
Pure smell of grass and dew. Now lantern-sheen
Falls on brown faces opening patient eyes
And lips of gentle answers, where each lies
Supine upon his stretcher, black of beard
Or with young cheeks; on caps and tunics smeared
And stained, white bandages round foot or head
Or arm, discoloured here and there with red.
Sons of all corners of wide France; from Lille,
Douay, the land beneath the invader's heel,
Champagne, Touraine, the fisher-villages
Of Brittany, the valleyed Pyrenees,
Blue coasts of the South, old Paris streets. Argonne
Of ever smouldering battle, that anon
Leaps furious, brothered them in arms. They fell
In the trenched forest scarred with reeking shell.
Now strange the sound comes round them in the night
Of English voices. By the wavering light
Quickly we have borne them, one by one, to the air,
And sweating in the dark lift up with care,
Tense-sinewed, each to his place. The cars at last
Complete their burden: slowly, and then fast
We glide away.

      And the dim round of sky,

Infinite and silent, broods unseeingly
Over the shadowy uplands rolling black
Into far woods, and the long road we track
Bordered with apparitions, as we pass,
Of trembling poplars and lamp-whitened grass,
A brief procession flitting like a thought
Through a brain drowsing into slumber; nought
But we awake in the solitude immense!
But hurting the vague dumbness of my sense
Are fancies wandering the night: there steals
Into my heart, like something that one feels
In darkness, the still presence of far homes
Lost in deep country, and in little rooms
The vacant bed. I touch the world of pain
That is so silent. Then I see again
Only those infinitely patient faces
In the lantern beam, beneath the night's vast spaces,
Amid the shadows and the scented dew;
And those illumined flowers, springing anew
In freshness like a smile of secrecy
From the gloom-buried earth, return to me.
The village sleeps; blank walls, and windows barred.
But lights are moving in the hushed courtyard
As we glide up to the open door. The Chief
Gives every man his order, prompt and brief.
We carry up our wounded, one by one.
The first cock crows: the morrow is begun.

The Ebb of War

In the seven-times taken and re-taken town
Peace! The mind stops; sense argues against sense.
The August sun is ghostly in the street
As if the Silence of a thousand years
Were its familiar. All is as it was
At the instant of the shattering: flat-thrown walls;
Dislocated rafters; lintels blown awry
And toppling over; what were windows, mere
Gapings on mounds of dust and shapelessness;
Charred posts caught in a bramble of twisted iron;
Wires sagging tangled across the street; the black
Skeleton of a vine, wrenched from the old house
It clung to; a limp bell-pull; here and there
Little printed papers pasted on the wall.
It is like a madness crumpled up in stone,
Laughterless, tearless, meaningless; a frenzy
Stilled, like at ebb the shingle in sea-caves
Where the imagined weight of water swung
Its senseless crash with pebbles in myriads churned
By the random seethe. But here was flesh and blood,
Seeing eyes, feeling nerves; memoried minds
With the habit of the picture of these fields
And the white roads crossing the wide green plain,
All vanished! One could fancy the very fields
Were memory's projection, phantoms! All
Silent! The stone is hot to the touching hand.
Footsteps come strange to the sense. In the sloped
      churchyard,
Where the tower shows the blue through its great rents,
Shadow falls over pitiful wrecked graves,
And on the gravel a bare-headed boy,

Hands in his pockets, with large absent eyes,
Whistles the Marseillaise: To Arms, To Arms!
There is no other sound in the bright air.
It is as if they heard under the grass,
The dead men of the Marne, and their thin voice
Used those young lips to sing it from their graves,
The song that sang a nation into arms.
And far away to the listening ear in the silence
Like remote thunder throb the guns of France.

The Sower

(Eastern France)
Familiar, year by year, to the creaking wain
Is the long road's level ridge above the plain.
To-day a battery comes with horses and guns
On the straight road, that under the poplars runs,
At leisurely pace, the guns with mouths declined,
Harness merrily ringing, and dust behind.
Makers of widows, makers of orphans, they
Pass to their burial business, alert and gay.

But down in the field, where sun has the furrow dried,
Is a man who walks in the furrow with even stride.
At every step, with elbow jerked across,
He scatters seed in a quick, deliberate toss,
The immemorial gesture of Man confiding
To Earth, that restores tenfold in a season's gliding.
He is grave and patient, sowing his children's bread:
He treads the kindly furrow, nor turns his head.

The Witnesses

I

Lads in the loose blue,
Crutched, with limping feet,
With bandaged arm, that roam
To-day the bustling street,

You humble us with your gaze,
Calm, confiding, clear;
You humble us with a smile
That says nothing but cheer.

Our souls are scarred with you!
Yet, though we suffered all
You have suffered, all were vain
To atone, or to recall

The robbed future, or build
The maimed body again
Whole, or ever efface
What men have done to men.

II

Each body of straight youth,
Strong, shapely, and marred,
Shines as out of a cloud
Of storm and splintered shard,

Of chaos, torture, blood,
Fire, thunder, and stench:
And the savage shattering noise
Of churned and shaken trench
Echoes through myriad hearts
In the dumb lands behind; –

Silent wailing, and bitter
Tears of the world's mind!

You stand upon each threshold
Without complaint. —What pen
Dares to write half the deeds
That men have done to men

III
Must we be humbled more?
Peace, whose olive seems
A tree of hope and heaven,
Of answered prayers and dreams,

Peace has her own hid wounds;
She also grinds and maims.
And must we bear and share
Those old continued shames?

Not only the body's waste
But the mind's captivities —
Crippled, sore, and starved —
The ignorant victories

Of the visionless, who serve
No cause, and fight no foe!
Is a cruelty less sure
Because its ways are slow?

Now we have eyes to see.
Shall we not use them then?
These bright wounds witness
What men may do to men.

Hunger

I come among the peoples like a shadow.
I sit down by each man's side.

None sees me, but they look on one another,
And know that I am there.

My silence is like the silence of the tide
That buries the playground of children;

Like the deepening of frost in the slow night,
When birds are dead in the morning.

Armies trample, invade, destroy,
With guns roaring from earth and air.

I am more terrible than armies,
I am more feared than the cannon.

Kings and chancellors give commands;
I give no command to any;

But I am listened to more than kings
And more than passionate orators.

I unswear words, and undo deeds.
Naked things know me.

I am first and last to be felt of the living.
I am Hunger.

The Arras Road

I

The early night falls on the plain
In cloud and desolating rain.
I see no more, but feel around
The ruined earth, the wounded ground.

There in the dark, on either side
The road, are all the brave who died.
I think not on the battles won;
I think on those whose day is done.

Heaped mud, blear pools, old rusted wire,
Cover their youth and young desire.
Near me they sleep, and they to me
Are dearer than their victory.

II

Where now are they who once had peace
Here, and the fruitful tilth's increase?
Shattered is all their hands had made,
And the orchards where their children played.

But night, that brings the darkness, brings
The heart back to its dearest things.
I feel old footsteps plodding slow
On ways that they were used to know.

And from my own land, past the strait,
From homes that no more news await,
Absenting thoughts come hither flying
To the unknown earth where Love is lying.

There are no stars to-night, but who
Knows what far eyes of lovers true
In star-like vigil, each alone
Are watching now above their own?

III

England and France unconscious tryst
Keep in this void of shadowy mist
By phantom Vimy, and mounds that tell
Of ghostliness that was Gavrelle.

The rain comes wildly down to drench
Disfeatured ridge, deserted trench.
Guns in the night, far, far away
Thud on the front beyond Cambrai.

But here the night is holy, and here
I will remember, and draw near,
And for a space, till night be sped,
Be with the beauty of the dead.

An Incident at Cambrai

In a by-street, blocked with rubble
And any-way-tumbled stones,
Between the upstanding house-fronts'
Naked and scorched bones,

Chinese workmen were clearing
The ruins, dusty and arid.
Dust whitened the motley coats,
Where each his burden carried.

Silent they glided, all
Save one, who passed me by
With berry-brown high-boned cheeks
And strange Eastern eye.

And he sang in his outland tongue
Among those ruins drear
A high, sad, half-choked ditty
That no one heeded to hear.

Was it love, was it grief, that made
For long-dead lips that song?
The desolation of Han
Or the Never-Ending Wrong?

The Rising Sun and the Setting,
They have seen this all as a scroll
Blood-smeared, that the endless years
For the fame of men unroll.

It was come from the ends of the earth
And of Time in his ruin gray,
That song, the one human sound
In the silence of Cambrai.

Wingless Victory

I

Victory! Was that proud word once so dear?
Are difficulty, patience, effort hard
As danger's edge, disputing yard by yard
The adversary without and the mind's fear,
Are these our only angels? friends austere
That find our hidden greatness out, and guard
From the weak hour's betrayal faith unmarred!
For look! how we seem fall'n from what we were.

Worms feed upon the bodies of the brave
Who bled for us: but we bewildered see
Viler worms gnaw the things they died to save.
Old clouds of doubt and weariness oppress.
Happy the dead, we cry, not now to be
In the day of this dissolving littleness!

II

O you dear Dead, pardon! For not resigned,
We see, though humbled, half our purpose bent
And our hope blurred, like men in banishment.
Giants amid a blank mist groping blind,
The nations ache. And old greeds unconfined
Possess men, sick at battle's blood hot-spent
Yet sleek and busy and righteously content
To wage war, safe and secret, on their kind.

If all were simple as the way of hate!
But we must reap where others sowed the seed
In time long past, of folly and pride and greed;
Confused with names, idols and polities;

Though over all earth, where we think a State,
There are but men and women; only these.

III
Victory, winged, has flown far off again.
She is in the soul, she travels with the light.
We see her on the distant mountain height
Desired, but she has left us in the plain,
Left us awhile, to chafe and to complain,
Yet keep our wills, in this dark time's despite,
Like those that went up to the horrible fight
Beneath their burdens, plodding in the rain.

Courage! The same stuff that so greatly bore
And greatly did, is here, for gods to find,
And the dear human cause in the heart's core.
Be the task always harder than we know,
And victory further, yet in pain we grow.
The vision is before us, not behind.

Pain

Find me out a fortress, find
Such a mind within the mind
As can gather to its source
All of life's inveterate force,
Find the hard and secret cell
In my body's citadel,
Iron-ribbed from suck and drain
Of the clutching monster, Pain –
Pain, the formless alien will
That seeks me out, that strives to drill
Through shielding thought and barricade
Of all the strength my will has made;
That singles me and searches through
The sharp sense I am narrowed to;
And ever as the bond I strain
Thrusts me home to flesh again,
Estranging me from earth, to be
One fierce throb of identity!
Yet there's fibre in the mind
I shall find, I shall find,
To resist and to defy
All the world that is not I.

Acknowledgements

Thanks and grateful acknowledgements are due to the copyright holders for their permission to include poems in the anthology as listed below. Also listed are the texts used for individual poems.

Ernest Hemingway, poems from *Complete Poems* edited by Nicholas Gerogiannis (University of Nebraska Press, 1992), reprinted by kind permission of the Ernest Hemingway Foundation.
Carola Oman, poems from *The Menin Road and Other Poems* (Hodder and Stoughton, 1919), reprinted by kind permission of Sir Roy Strong.
May Cannan, poems from *In War Time* (Blackwell, 1917) and *The Splendid Days* (Blackwell, 1919), reprinted by kind permission of Clara Abrahams and the May Wedderburn Cannan Estate.
E.E. Cummings, poems from *Complete Poems 1904 – 1962*, edited by George J Firmage, Introduction by Stephen Dunn (Liveright, 2016). "the bigness of cannon". Copyright 1923, 1951, (c) 1991 by the Trustees for the E. E. Cummings Trust. Copyright (c) 1976 by George James Firmage, "first she like a piece of ill-oiled". Copyright © 1973, 1983, 1991 by the Trustees for the E. E. Cummings Trust. Copyright (c) 1973, 1983 by George James Firmage, "it's jolly". Copyright 1926, 1954, (c) 1991 by the Trustees for the E. E. Cummings Trust. Copyright (c) 1985 by George James Firmage, "lis". Copyright 1926, 1954, (c) 1991 by the Trustees for the E. E. Cummings Trust. Copyright (c) 1985 by George James Firmage, "look at this)". Copyright 1926, 1954, (c) 1991 by the Trustees for the E. E.Cummings Trust. Copyright (c) 1985 by George James Firmage, "my sweet old etcetera". Copyright 1926, 1954,(c) 1991 by the Trustees for the E. E. Cummings Trust. Copyright (c) 1985 by George James Firmage, "next to of course god america i". Copyright 1926, 1954, (c) 1991 by the Trustees for the E. E. Cummings Trust. Copyright (c) 1985 by George James Firmage, "O sweet spontaneous". Copyright 1923, 1951, (c) 1991 by the Trustees for the E. E. Cummings Trust. Copyright (c) 1976 by George James Firmage, from COMPLETE POEMS: 1904-1962 by E. E. Cummings, edited by George J. Firmage. Used by permission of Liveright Publishing Corporation.
Vera Brittain, poems from *Because You Died: Poetry and Prose of the*

First World War and After, Edited and Introduced by Mark Bostridge (Virago, 2008), reprinted by kind permission of Mark Bostridge and TJ Brittain-Catlin, Literary Executors for the Estate of Vera Brittain 1970.

Mary Borden, poems from *Poems of Love and War*, edited by Paul O'Prey (Dare-Gale Press, 2015) reprinted by kind permission of Patrick Aylmer.

Geoffrey Studdert Kennedy, poems from *The Unutterable Beauty, The Collected Poetry of G.A. Studdert Kennedy* (Hodder and Stoughton, 1927).

John Masefield, poems from *John Masefield's Great War*, edited by Philip W Errington (Pen and Sword, 2007), reprinted by kind permission of the Society of Authors as Literary Representative of the Estate of John Masefield.

Robert Service, poems from *Collected Poems* (GP Putnam's Sons, 1989) reprinted by kind permission of Anne Longepe and Charlotte Service-Longpepe, and the Robert Service Estate.

Laurence Binyon, poems from *Poems of Two Wars*, edited by Paul O'Prey (Dare-Gale Press, 2016) reprinted by kind permission of the Society of Authors as Literary Representative of the Estate of Laurence Binyon.